Charlie Brown's
ENCYCLOPEDIA OF
ENERGY

Charlie Brown's ENCYCLOPEDIA OF ENERGY

Based on the Charles M. Schulz Characters

where we've been,

where we're going

and how we're getting there

Random House  New York

Editor: Hedda Nussbaum
Art Director: Eleanor Ehrhardt
Designer: Terry Flanagan
Graphics: Roberta Pressel
Layout: Charlotte Staub
Production: Elaine Silber

Special thanks to:

Daniel Halacy
Solar Energy Research Institute

Dr. Ira Freeman
Science Consultant,
Former Professor of Physics
Rutgers University

Photograph and illustration credits: W. K. Almond/Stock, Boston, 50 right; © Arthur d'Arazien/The Image Bank, 18 left; © Charles R. Belinky/Photo Researchers, Inc., 44 top right; Berkey K & L, 71 bottom; Gerald Brimacombe/The Image Bank, 99 bottom; © Vincent Camagna/Stock, Boston, 104 right; Michael Collier/Stock, Boston, 45 bottom right; © Donald Dietz/Stock, Boston, 33; Terry Flanagan, 110; Owen Franken/Stock, Boston, 63, 74; © David Frazier/Photo Researchers, Inc., 71; © Peter Frey/The Image Bank, 45 bottom left; Bill Gillette/Stock, Boston, 76 bottom right, 105; © Larry Gordon/The Image Bank, 77 top; Edith G. Haun/Stock, Boston, 75 top; Marty Heitner/Taurus Photos, 75 bottom; © Eric Kroll/Taurus Photos, 18 right, 19 bottom, 21, 76 bottom left, 77 bottom, 95; © Tom McHugh/Photo Researchers, Inc., 43, 44 top left, 97; Peter Menzel/Stock, Boston, 96; © Al Michaud/The Image Bank, 19 top; National Aeronautics and Space Administration, 89, 102; Occidental Petroleum/The Image Bank, 76 top; L.L.T. Rhodes/Taurus Photos, 50 left; © Earl Roberge/Photo Researchers, Inc., 69; Harold Roth, 79; John Running/Stock, Boston, 104 left; © Carol Simowitz/The Image Bank, 52; The Bettmann Archive, Inc., 4, 8, 16, 25, 26, 30, 35, 51, 54, 62, 90; The Granger Collection, 59, 61, 82, 99 top, 107, 108; © Thomas R. Taylor/Photo Researchers, Inc., 44 bottom, 45 top; © Peter Turner/The Image Bank, 55; United Press International, 56, 81, 92; United States Department of Energy, 6.

Cover photo: © 1978 Rafael Macia/Photo Researchers, Inc.

Library of Congress Cataloging in Publication Data:
Main entry under title: Charlie Brown's encyclopedia of energy. Includes index. SUMMARY: Alphabetically arranged entries dealing with aspects of energy including fuels, famous people, and types of energy. 1. Power resources—Dictionaries—Juvenile literature. [1. Power resources—Dictionaries] I. Schulz, Charles M. II. Nussbaum, Hedda [date]
TJ163.23.C45   333.79'03'21   AACR2   82-3767   ISBN: 0-394-84682-6   ISBN: 0-394-94682-0 (lib. bdg.)
Manufactured in the United States of America   1 2 3 4 5 6 7 8 9 0

Introduction

Thousands of years ago, all work was done by humans or animals. Today, in industrialized countries, most work is done by machines. This makes life easier, and lets us do things like fly across the country in a few hours. Machines, however, need energy—not food energy, like we humans use, but energy that comes from fuels like oil and gas. Now those fuels are getting scarce and very expensive. Someday they will be used up completely. Then what will we do? And what can we do now to prepare ourselves?

We have two choices: We can slowly change our life style back to the way it was thousands of years ago, or we can find new sources of energy. The second choice seems better. With effort, we can make new kinds of fuels in factories. Better yet, we can use energy sources that will never run out—the sun, the wind, water, and wood and other renewable fuels.

Our energy future is challenging but interesting too. If we start now to explore new energy sources, someday we will not only have all the energy we need—it will be safe, clean energy as well.

Abbot, Charles Greeley

Dr. Charles G. Abbot was America's first solar scientist. He was born in New Hampshire in 1872, and studied science in school. Later, he went to work for the Smithsonian Institution in Washington, D.C. As part of his scientific research there, he measured the amount of energy that reaches the earth from the sun. He also studied sunspots. He learned how they change our weather.

Dr. Abbot built solar cookers, or stoves, and made engines that run on sunshine. He patented many inventions. He was still inventing when he died at age 102!

See Solar Constant; Solar Cooker; Sunspots

Air Pollution. See Pollution

Alpha Rays. See Nuclear Radiation

Alternating Current

Alternating current is electricity that flows first in one direction and then in the opposite. In 1882 Thomas Edison built one of the first two electric power plants in the United States. A power plant is a place where electric current is generated. Edison used current flowing in only one direction to light lamps and run appliances. But other scientists, including Charles Steinmetz, proved that alternating current works better.

The electric current in your home changes direction 120 times every second! The current moves back and forth in the wires like a handsaw does cutting wood.

See Direct Current; Edison, Thomas Alva; Steinmetz, Charles Proteus

Alternative Energy Sources

Alternative energy sources are new and different places and things that can produce energy. The world is running out of oil and gas. And not much uranium is left for nuclear power plants. So scientists and engineers are looking for other sources of energy and ways to use them.

A new kind of fuel called synthetic (sin-THEH-tick) fuel is being made from a type of rock called oil shale. Oil shale is an alternative energy source. So are ocean waves and ocean tides. Heat escaping from deep inside the earth is still another source. But the best alternative is solar energy—energy from the sun. It is always available. And it will not run out for billions of years!

See Geothermal Energy; Nuclear Power Plant; Oil Shale; Solar Energy; Synthetic Fuels; Wave Power; Windmill

SURE, BIRDS GET ENERGY FROM THE SUN TOO!

Alternator

There is a round metal device under the hood of your car called an alternator. It changes mechanical energy into electrical energy that goes into your car's battery. Electricity runs the starter, the lights, and other equipment in your car. A few years back, a simpler device called a generator was used. But the alternator does a better job.

See Electric Generator

American Petroleum Institute

The American Petroleum Institute (API) looks for new and better ways to make and use oil products. API was started in 1919. Its people pass along information about oil to the government, the oil industry, and anyone who uses oil.

See Oil

Ampère, André Marie

André Ampère (AM-peer) was one of the first people to study electricity. He was born in France in 1775. Ampère became a mathematician when he was only 12 years old. The emperor Napoleon encouraged the bright young man in his studies of mathematics, chemistry, and physics.

Ampère became interested in electricity. He discovered how electricity flows through wires. Ampère (and Benjamin Franklin too!) thought electrical current flowed opposite to the way it really does. But Ampère is respected as a pioneer in the science of electricity. In his honor, electric current is measured in amperes.

See Electric Current; Franklin, Benjamin

I THINK WE COULD BE GREAT MATHEMATICIANS TOO, MARCIE. ALL WE NEED IS A POCKET COMPUTER.

André Ampère

Anthracite. See Coal

Atom

All things are made of tiny bits of matter called atoms. They are so tiny that they can't even be seen with most microscopes. The ancient Greek scientist Democritus (duh-MOCK-ruh-tuss) thought that these bits of matter must be solid. He named them atoms. In Greek, *atom* meant something that can't be divided. But modern scientists have found that the atom is really made up of even tinier particles. In the center of an atom is the nucleus, made up of particles called neutrons and protons. Around the nucleus whiz a third kind of particle called electrons.

See Dalton, John; Democritus; Electron; Neutron; Nucleus

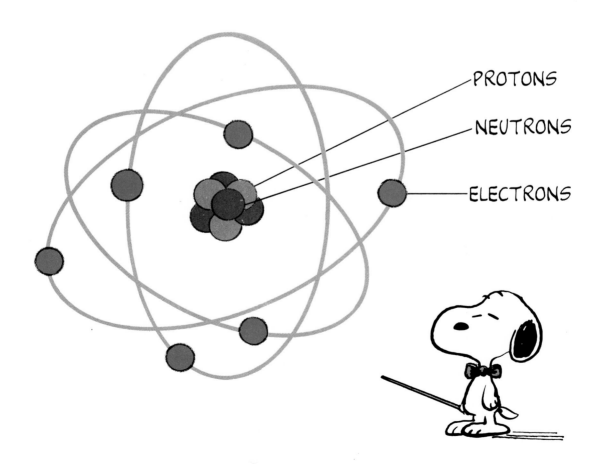

PROTONS

NEUTRONS

ELECTRONS

Atomic Bomb

An atomic bomb is exploded by the splitting of atoms. The first atomic bomb was exploded as a test, at Alamogordo, New Mexico, in 1945. Uranium was used to make the atomic bomb. The splitting of many uranium atoms released unbelievable amounts of energy. A few pounds of uranium made as big an explosion as 20,000 tons of ordinary explosives!

Atomic bombs dropped on the Japanese cities of Hiroshima and Nagasaki in 1945 quickly ended World War II. Since that time, no atomic bombs have been used in warfare.

See Atom; Uranium

Atomic Energy. See Nuclear Energy

Atomic Energy Commission

In 1946, after World War II was over, the U.S. government set up the Atomic Energy Commission (AEC). The AEC took charge of all work with nuclear energy until 1974. Then Congress set up the Energy Research and Development Administration (ERDA). ERDA did all the work of the AEC, except for one thing. It could not make rules or watch over nuclear power plants. The Nuclear Regulatory Commission did that. And it still does.

See Department of Energy; Nuclear Regulatory Commission

Atomic Reactor. See Nuclear Reactor

Atoms for Peace

Atoms for Peace was a program developed to show that the power of the atom could be used for good—not just for bombs. In 1954 President Dwight D. Eisenhower made Atoms for Peace a national goal. He wanted nuclear energy to be used for mining, to produce electric power, for scientific research, and even to cure cancer.

Atom Splitting

Splitting an atom lets out some of the energy that holds the atom together. In 1919 scientist Ernest Rutherford was able to split an atom of nitrogen. Twenty years later German scientists split a uranium atom. Uranium is a radioactive material—one whose atoms are always splitting, but at a very slow rate. This natural splitting can be sped up artificially. When a lot of uranium is put together, there is a chain reaction of rapidly splitting atoms. Then great amounts of energy come from the uranium. In 1942, Enrico Fermi made the first atomic chain reaction. Artificial atom splitting was the beginning of the nuclear age.

See Chain Reaction; Fermi, Enrico; Nuclear Energy; Radioactivity; Rutherford, Ernest

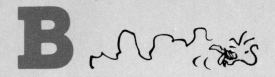

B

Battery. See Electric Battery

Becquerel, Henri

Henri Becquerel (beck-uh-RELL) was a French scientist whose experiments led to the discovery of radioactivity. He was born in 1852 in Paris. In 1896 he experimented with the effects of sunlight on a certain radioactive material. But he did not know it was radioactive. No one knew about radioactivity yet. Becquerel accidentally discovered that the material was sending out energy. This energy was much like the X-rays that Wilhelm Konrad Roentgen had recently discovered. Other scientists did more research on what was now called the Becquerel effect. From this research came the discovery of radioactivity.

Becquerel received the 1903 Nobel prize in physics for his discovery. The Nobel prize is the highest possible award a scientist can get. Becquerel shared the award with Marie and Pierre Curie, who had continued his research.

See Curie, Marie and Pierre; Radioactivity; Roentgen, Wilhelm Konrad

Henri Becquerel in his laboratory

Bioconversion

The process of bioconversion (BY-o-kun-VUR-shun) changes biomass (plant and animal matter) to fuels. These fuels can take the place of natural gas and gasoline, which are getting scarce.

Tiny living things called bacteria (back-TEER-ee-uh) change sewage and other wastes to a gas called methane (MEH-thane). This is much like natural gas (except it is smellier!) and can be burned as fuel. Chemicals called enzymes (EN-zimes) can change corn, grains, and other plants into alcohol. Alcohol is also used as a fuel. Because there will always be new plants and new garbage, biomass will never run out.

See **Biomass; Gasohol; Methane**

Biomass

Biomass includes all the living things in the world. But the word biomass is generally used to mean plant matter.

Plant biomass gives us many of the things we need to live. It gives us food (fruits, vegetables, and grains). It gives us clothing (cotton and linen). And today, more than ever, biomass is providing people with fuel (wood, fossil fuels, methane gas, and alcohol).

See **Bioconversion; Fossil Fuels**

Blackout

A blackout occurs when electric power plants fail. Our lights and all our electrical appliances go off. In summer, when air conditioners use a great deal of power, the supply sometimes runs out. Winter heating loads can also cause blackouts.

Our electric power comes from huge networks of power lines, called grids. Electricity may travel hundreds of miles. So a power failure in one state can cause a blackout in other states.

See Brownout; Electric Power

Blast Wave

A blast wave is caused by the explosion of an atomic bomb. Such an explosion makes a great deal of heat. Air is expanded by this heat, and it rushes out in all directions. This strong, hot wind is the blast wave. It flattens nearly everything in its path.

See Atomic Bomb

Bohr, Niels

Niels Bohr was a famous nuclear scientist. He helped develop nuclear science for use in both war and peace. Bohr was born in Copenhagen, Denmark, in 1885. At school, he played soccer and studied physics. Bohr was good at soccer but even better at science. In 1922 he received the Nobel prize for his theory of what was inside a hydrogen atom. He also proved that atoms are not solid bits of matter but instead are made of many tinier parts.

Bohr came to the United States in 1939 and helped develop the first atomic bomb. In 1955 he organized the first Atoms for Peace conference. Two years later he received the first Atoms for Peace award.

See Atom; Atoms for Peace

Breeder Reactor

A breeder reactor is a special kind of nuclear reactor. Like most nuclear reactors, it uses uranium as fuel. But what makes a breeder reactor special is that not all the uranium gets used up. Instead, some of it is changed into something new—plutonium. The plutonium can be taken from the breeder reactor and used for fuel in other reactors.

Plutonium is a more dangerous fuel than uranium because it is more radioactive. Also, its halflife is longer, and it can more easily be used to make atomic bombs.

France and some other countries run breeder reactors to produce electric power. But the U.S. government does not. It believes that the plutonium might be stolen and used to make bombs.

See Atomic Bomb; Halflife; Nuclear Reactor; Plutonium; Radioactivity; Uranium

POWER PLANT
NO
UNAUTHORIZED
PERSONNEL

Brownout

A brownout is a weakening of our electric power supply. It is not as bad as a blackout, where all the lights go out. But the lights dim, and motors run slowly. A motor may be damaged by running at low power. Brownouts are caused the same way that blackouts are — by too little electricity to take care of all our needs.

See Blackout

HOW ROMANTIC... A LOAF OF BREAD, A JUG OF ROOT BEER, AND THOU — IN A BROWNOUT.

Btu

A Btu is a British thermal unit, used to measure heat energy. One Btu will raise the temperature of one pound of water one degree Fahrenheit (FAIR-un-hite). Burning one match makes about one Btu of heat.

Your furnace or air conditioner probably has a Btu rating stamped on it. The furnace puts a certain amount of heat energy into the air each hour. The air conditioner takes a certain amount of heat energy out of the air each hour. These amounts are measured in Btus.

See Fahrenheit, Gabriel Daniel; Heat Energy

Butane

Butane is a gas made from oil. It can be compressed (squeezed into a small space) so that a lot of energy can fit into a little tank. Butane is used mostly for heating, but it can also run a car or a truck. Sometimes it is used for lamps, stoves, and cigarette lighters as well.

See Oil Refinery; Propane

Calorie

A calorie is a measure of heat energy. One calorie can raise the temperature of one cubic centimeter of water one degree Celsius. This is a gram calorie, or small calorie. It is used in heat engineering.

A large calorie is also called a kilogram calorie. It is equal to 1,000 small calories. Large calories are used in measuring food value. Large calories are the kind that make us large!

See Celsius

Carbon

Carbon is a chemical element that is part of all living things. There is carbon in carbohydrates, the sugars and starches we eat. Because oil, coal, and natural gas were once plants (millions of years ago), they also contain carbon.

See Element (Chemical); Fossil Fuels; Hydrocarbons

Carbon Dioxide

Carbon dioxide is a gas made of carbon and oxygen. Carbon dioxide is used in fire extinguishers. Frozen carbon dioxide, called dry ice, keeps things cold.

When wood, coal, gas, and oil (called fossil fuel) burn, they give off invisible carbon dioxide. Some scientists think we are putting so much carbon dioxide into the air, that it is forming a screen that keeps heat inside. So the atmosphere may be heating up slowly. The time may come when we will have to stop burning so much fossil fuel.

See Fossil Fuels

Carboniferous Period (The Coal Age)

The Carboniferous (kar-buh-NIFF-ur-us) Period was a time many millions of years ago when coal was formed. Over hundreds of millions of years, rotted plants slowly changed to coal. The pressure of water, rock, and soil over the plant matter squeezed the plants into the hard, black form that we call coal.

See Coal; Fossil Fuels

IT'S COMFORTING TO KNOW THAT MY ROTTED RADISHES MAY BE TOMORROW'S COAL.

Carbon Monoxide

Carbon monoxide is a gas made of carbon and oxygen. These are the same chemical elements that make up carbon dioxide, but in different amounts. Unlike carbon dioxide, carbon monoxide is a deadly poison. Some of it comes from the exhaust pipes of car engines. Wherever there is a lot of traffic, there is also a lot of carbon monoxide pollution in the air.

See Carbon Dioxide

Carnot, Nicolas Léonard Sadi

Nicolas Carnot (kar-NOE) was a French scientist who studied heat energy. He was born in Paris in 1796. He began his career as an engineer in the army. Later, he became a scientist. His book, ON THE MOTIVE POWER OF FIRE, began the science of thermodynamics (thur-moe-dye-NAM-icks), or heat energy. Carnot showed that the efficiency of a heat engine (how well it performs) depends on how hot it is.

Unfortunately, Carnot died when he was only 36. But other scientists continued his work and finished writing the laws of thermodynamics. The Carnot cycle, which describes how a heat engine works, was named for him.

See Efficiency; Heat Energy

HE THINKS WE SHOULD BRING BACK THE HORSE AND BUGGY...

Anders Celsius

Chadwick, James

James Chadwick was a scientist who discovered tiny particles in atoms called neutrons. He was born in Lancashire, England, in 1891. At age 20 he began to work with scientist Ernest Rutherford. After many years of research, Chadwick received the Nobel prize in physics for discovering the neutron.

During World War II, Chadwick headed the atomic bomb project in Great Britain. In 1945 the king of England made Chadwick a knight to honor his work.

See Neutron; Rutherford, Ernest

Celsius, Anders

Anders Celsius (SELL-see-us) was a Swedish scientist who invented a temperature scale used by a large part of the world. He was born in Uppsala, Sweden, in 1701. Celsius was an astronomer, but we remember him for his way of measuring temperature. He used 0 degrees (°) for the point where water freezes, and 100° for the point where it boils. For many years this was called the Centigrade scale. But now it is known as the Celsius scale.

See Fahrenheit, Gabriel Daniel

Chain Reaction

A chain reaction is something that keeps going by itself—like dominoes falling. Uranium has a natural chain reaction that goes on inside its atoms. If enough uranium is put together, the chain reaction can speed up and cause an atomic explosion.

See Atomic Bomb; Uranium

The clean air act is a good thing because if the air is clean we kids wont have to bathe so much.

Pig Pen

Clean Air Act

The Clean Air Act set up a law against polluting the atmosphere. England passed this law in 1956, the United States in 1970. Now power plants have to clean up the smoke from their smokestacks. And we have smog-control devices on our cars, trucks, and buses.

The Clean Air Act is making skies clearer. More important, it makes clearer, purer air for humans and animals to breathe.

See Pollution

Coal

Coal is a kind of burnable rock. More than half its weight is carbon. The rest is minerals and moisture. Coal was made from rotted plant life many millions of years ago. First an ancient swamp was buried for ages. Chemical action and the pressure of rocks that covered the plant life changed it slowly to coal.

When plants turn to coal, they first become peat, a mushy but burnable substance. The peat becomes lignite, brown coal. This slowly changes to bituminous (buh-TOO-muh-nuss) or soft coal. Finally it becomes anthracite (AN-thruh-site), or hard coal.

There is enough coal in the United States to last a few hundred more years. But it took about 600 million years for it to form!

See Carboniferous Period; Fossil Fuels

Coal Mining

The first coal was mined, or dug, close to the surface of the earth. As more coal was needed, miners had to dig deeper into the ground. This is hard, dangerous work. The many caves and tunnels of the mine must be kept from caving in. Fresh air is needed to keep the miners alive and healthy.

See Coal; Strip Mining

A conveyer system brings coal to a storage and transfer terminal.

Coal moving along a conveyer belt into a shuttle car

A coal preparation plant, where coal is cleaned

A modern mining machine works much faster than a miner with a pick.

Cogeneration

The word cogeneration (koe-jen-uh-RAY-shun) comes from two Latin words that mean creating together. In a power plant, fuel is burned to generate power. But only about one-third of that fuel's energy becomes power. Usually, the other two-thirds are wasted. Today, some power plants are using the waste energy to heat water and buildings. That use is called cogeneration.

Cogeneration is used a lot in Europe. Now it is becoming popular in the United States, too.
See Conservation

Coke

The kind of coke talked about in an energy book has nothing to do with soft drinks. Coke is a very pure form of coal. It is made by heating coal in an oven. The coal gets very hot until ammonia and tar are burned off. The remaining substance is called coke. It is burned when ore is made into iron and steel.

Combustion

Combustion is the burning of fuel. The carbon and hydrogen in fuel mix with oxygen in the air. Combustion makes heat. It may also make smoke and other things that pollute the air.
See Fuel

Compressor Station

A compressor station is a pump. It forces oil or gas through a pipeline. Pumping is the cheapest way to move oil and gas across long distances.

Concentrating Solar Collector

A concentrating solar collector puts lots of solar energy into a small area. This creates a very high temperature—hot enough to make steam to run an engine. Flat or curved mirrors make good concentrating solar collectors.

See Flat-Plate Solar Collector; Power Tower

Conduction of Heat

Conduction (kun-DUCK-shun) is one way in which heat can move through matter. Heat moves readily through iron and aluminum. So these metals are good conductors of heat. But heat moves with great difficulty through air, which is a bad conductor. Air is a good insulator (IN-suh-lay-tur). So anything that traps air makes good insulation. And good insulation keeps our homes warm in winter and cool in summer.

Conservation

Conservation means saving something. Right now we are especially interested in saving energy. This is called energy conservation.

WAYS TO SAVE ENERGY
1. Turn off the lights when you leave a room.
2. In winter, keep the temperature of your house at 68 degrees Fahrenheit (20° Celsius) during the day. At night keep it at 60° F (16° C).
   In summer, keep the air conditioner set at 78° F (26° C).
3. Walk or ride your bike instead of asking your parents to drive you everywhere.
4. Encourage the grownups you know to insulate their homes better.

Can you think of any other ways to save energy?

Continental Shelf

A continental shelf is part of a continent that is under the ocean. Each continent (North America and Africa, for example) has a rim of underwater land that borders its coastline. Close to shore, the water is shallow because of the continental shelf. A continental shelf extends for many miles. Then it ends, and the underwater land drops steeply to the deep ocean floor.

Because of the shallower water, oil and natural gas are easier to reach in the continental shelves than in the middle of the ocean.

See Natural Gas; Oil

Core Drilling

Core drilling takes samples of the sand or earth that an oil well drill is cutting through. Drillers use special core drills to cut out the samples. These core samples tell if there is oil or gas at a given distance down the well.

See Oil Well

Critical Mass

Critical mass is a term used in talking about a nuclear reactor. The critical mass is just enough atomic fuel to cause a chain reaction. A nuclear reactor must have exactly the right amount of fuel. Too little, and the reactor doesn't get hot enough. Too much, and the reactor may overheat, or even melt down.

See Chain Reaction; Meltdown; Nuclear Reactor

WELL, THERE IS A CRITICAL MASS AND THEN THERE IS A CRITICAL MASS...

Crude Oil

Crude oil is petroleum as it comes from the oil well. When oil was first discovered, it was burned in this form. Now factories called oil refineries change crude oil into many different fuels and other products. Gasoline, gasohol, kerosene, heating oil, and motor oil are examples.

See Oil Refinery

Curie, Marie and Pierre

Marie and Pierre Curie were scientists. They became famous for discovering the element called radium.

Pierre Curie was born in Paris in 1859. Marie Sklodowska (skluh-DOW-skuh) was born in Warsaw, Poland, in 1867. She and Pierre met in France and married in 1895. They experimented with uranium. Marie gave the name radioactivity to the radiation it gives off.

The Curies also discovered the element called polonium. (They named it for Poland.) Polonium is much more radioactive than uranium.

Marie Curie in her laboratory

In 1903 the Curies received the Nobel prize in physics. Marie received a second Nobel prize in 1911. Pierre was killed in Paris by a runaway horse. Marie died in 1934 of cancer caused by her exposure to radioactive material.

See **Curium; Element (Chemical); Radioactivity; Radium**

Curium

Curium is a powerfully radioactive element. It is made from plutonium and uranium, and is 3,000 times as radioactive as radium. Curium is named for Marie and Pierre Curie.

See **Element (Chemical); Plutonium; Radioactivity; Radium; Uranium**

D

Dalton, John

John Dalton was first to say that atoms are not solid bits of matter. He was born in Cumberland, England, in 1766. He left school at the age of 12 to become a teacher! Later he studied chemistry.

In 1803 Dalton suggested a new theory for the atom. He said that the tiny atoms are made of even smaller particles. This theory was different from the old one that said atoms are solid. But most scientists soon accepted Dalton's theory.

See Atom; Democritus

John Dalton

MUSEUM OF SCIENCE

D'Arsonval, Jacques Arsène

Jacques d'Arsonval (zhock DAHR-sun-vahl) was a French scientist born in 1851. He invented a machine that measures electric current.

D'Arsonval was the first person to suggest using the tremendous heat energy in the oceans. He thought that an engine could run on that heat. D'Arsonval did not prove his theory with an actual engine. But a student of his, Georges Claude, built one in Cuba in 1929. It was a failure. But successful ocean heat engines are being built today.

See Electric Current; Ocean Thermal Energy Conversion

Democritus

Democritus (duh-MOCK-ruh-tus) was an ancient Greek scientist born about 500 years before Christ. He was called the laughing philosopher because he was so cheerful. Democritus gave the name atoms to what he thought were the tiniest bits of matter. The word atom meant undividable in ancient Greek. For years people believed that atoms could not be divided. In fact, more than two thousand years passed before it was learned that atoms were not the smallest building blocks of nature. Now we know that atoms are made of a number of much tinier parts.

See **Atom; Dalton, John**

Department of Energy

The U.S. Department of Energy (DOE) was formed in 1977 to help solve energy problems in America. DOE replaced the Energy Research and Development Administration (ERDA). One job of DOE is to see that the United States saves energy by conservation. Another job is to find new sources of energy.

See **Energy Research and Development Administration**

Deuterium

Deuterium (doo-TEER-ee-um) is a special form of hydrogen. Its atoms are heavier than those of ordinary hydrogen. Hydrogen and oxygen combine chemically to form water. Deuterium and oxygen form heavy water. This is used in some nuclear reactors to help get a chain reaction started. Deuterium itself may be the fuel for future nuclear fusion reactors.

See Atom; Hydrogen; Nuclear Fusion; Nuclear Reactor

Diesel Engine

A diesel (DEE-zul) engine runs on fuel that is cheaper than gasoline. Many trains, buses, trucks, and even cars have diesel engines. This kind of engine does not need spark plugs the way a gasoline engine does. And it gets more miles to the gallon than a gasoline engine does. So it is becoming more popular as the cost of fuel goes up. Cars from Volkswagens to Cadillacs use diesel engines now.

The engine was named for the man who invented it in 1897 — Rudolph Diesel of Germany.

Direct Current

Direct current is electricity flowing in only one direction. A battery produces direct current. So does a bolt of lightning.
See Alternating Current

Dynamo. See Electric Generator

THERE, THERE, LITTLE FRIEND. THE STORM IS ALMOST OVER.

SNIF

E

Ecology

Ecology is the science of how all living things get along in the environment. The word was invented by a German scientist, Ernst Haeckel (HECK-ul). He combined the Greek words *oikos* (household) and *logos* (study of). And so ecology is, in a way, the study of the whole world as a household.

I THINK I SEE SOME PUFFY BIRDS, SIR!

THOSE AREN'T "PUFFY BIRDS," MARCIE, THOSE ARE CLOUDS!

Edison, Thomas Alva

Thomas Edison was America's greatest inventor. He was born in Milan, Ohio, in 1847. Young Tom was so curious about things that his teachers said he was strange. So his mother took him out of school. He learned from books at home.

Tom studied electricity and then began to invent things. He was 21 when he made his first invention. Not long after that, he started a laboratory in Menlo Park, New Jersey. A great many people worked for him. There Edison invented the phonograph, movies, and many more things. He patented 1,300 inventions! Edison gave us two very important energy inventions—the electric light and the large electric power plant that serves a whole community.

Thomas Edison

Efficiency

Efficiency (uh-FISH-un-see) is a measure of how much work a machine does for the amount of energy it uses. All machines waste some energy in heat, noise, and friction (the rubbing of one part against another). A large electric power plant is one of the most efficient machines. But it changes only about 38 percent of the energy in its fuel to power. So the power plant is 38 percent efficient.

Fuel is becoming scarce and expensive. So we must learn to build more efficient machines to make our fuel go further.

See Cogeneration; Conservation

Einstein, Albert

Albert Einstein may have been the smartest scientist who ever lived. He was born in Germany in 1879. He liked mathematics in school. But he didn't seem very smart. He became a clerk. On his own, he began to study such things as gravity, electricity, and magnetism. When he was 26 years old he proved how smart he was. He published his ideas in a famous paper. Years later this won Einstein the Nobel prize in physics.

Einstein changed our ideas about time and space. He also showed that matter could be changed to energy. From this came the theory of the atomic bomb. In fact, it was Einstein who asked President Franklin D. Roosevelt to develop the atomic bomb.

The chemical element einsteinium was named in honor of Einstein.

See Atomic Bomb; Matter and Energy

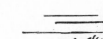

Electric Battery

A battery produces and stores up electrical energy. Electric current is generated when chemicals react with each other.

A flashlight battery is a good example. Inside a little can made of zinc is a carbon rod. Ammonium chloride (uh-MOE-nee-um KLOHR-ide) paste fills up the can. The ammonium chloride causes the carbon and zinc to react. Their electrons start moving around. When this happens, an electric current is produced. It flows between the carbon and the zinc.

Your car battery uses two kinds of chemicals—lead and lead peroxide (instead of carbon and zinc). These chemicals are in the form of solid plates. There is a sulfuric (sull-FYOOR-ick) acid mixture around the plates. The acid makes the plate materials react. When all the chemical energy from the plates has changed to electric current, the battery is dead. Then a battery charger can be used to reverse the chemical reaction. So, unlike a flashlight battery, which cannot be recharged, this battery can once again store up chemical energy. Now it can start the engine and run the lights again.

See Electron

Electric Car

An electric car runs on electricity instead of gasoline. It uses many electric batteries, and an electric motor instead of a gasoline engine. Electric cars were running before Henry Ford built his first gasoline-powered car in 1908. But gasoline-powered cars could go much farther without stopping than electric cars could. So gasoline-powered cars became popular and the use of electric cars died out.

Today electric cars are being built again. They don't pollute the air. They don't make much noise. And their fuel is cheap. Once electric cars are improved, they may take the place of gasoline-engine cars.

See Electric Battery

Electric Circuit

An electric circuit is a path for electricity. Circuit means that the wires form a complete, closed loop. This circuit goes from the electric battery or power plant to lights, stoves, refrigerators, etc., and back to the battery or power plant.

See Electric Battery; Electric Current; Electric Generator

BEEP BEEP...

Electric Current

An electric current is a stream of electricity. The current in a wire consists of electrons moving among the atoms of the wire.
See Atom; Electron

Electric Eel

An electric eel is a South American fish that really produces electricity. It can generate enough electricity to light a neon bulb, or to shock its enemies or the fish it is trying to eat. So electricity isn't made just by batteries or generators. The kind made by living things is called bioelectricity (BY-oh-uh-leck-TRISS-uh-tee).

Electric Generator

An electric generator is a machine that produces electric power in a power plant. It is sometimes called a dynamo. The generator has a moving part called a rotor. It spins inside a part called a stator.

Basically, an electric generator changes mechanical energy into electrical energy. The mechanical energy comes from the work needed to turn the rotor. A steam engine or water turbine usually supplies this work.

See Turbine; Work

Electricity

Electricity is a kind of natural energy caused by the flow of tiny parts of atoms called electrons. All matter is made up of atoms. And all atoms have electrons in them. Some kinds of atoms have electrons that are loosely attached, and they can easily be made to move from one atom to another. When electrons move among the atoms of matter, a current of electricity is created. This electric current lights lamps and runs TV sets and many other appliances.

See Atom; Electron

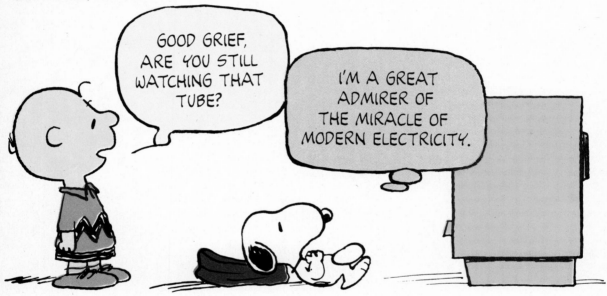

Electric Power

The production of electric currents in a power plant is sometimes called electric power. It lights our homes. It runs radios and TV sets. Electricity also powers factories and some trains.

Electric Power Research Institute

The Electric Power Research Institute (EPRI) develops better ways to make and use electric power. It was started in 1972 in Palo Alto, California. Now more than 500 men and women work there. They do research on nuclear energy, fossil fuels, and solar energy.

See Fossil Fuels; Nuclear Energy; Solar Energy

Electromagnetic Radiation

Electromagnetic (ih-LECK-troe-mag-NET-ick) radiation is energy in the form of electric and magnetic waves. The sun gives off lots of electromagnetic radiation. So do radio transmitters, x-ray machines, and radioactive materials.

See Radiation

Electron

Electrons are parts of all atoms. You can think of them whizzing around the atom's nucleus, its center. They move faster than you can imagine—more than 100 times faster than many jet planes fly! Sometimes electrons move among the atoms of a wire. This movement is electric current.

See Atom; Nucleus (Atomic)

Element (Chemical)

A chemical element is matter made of only one kind of atom. Iron contains only iron atoms. Oxygen has only oxygen atoms. Scientists have discovered 103 different elements, including several man-made types. The elements are the building blocks that make up the world and the universe.

See Atom

Energy

Energy is the ability to do work. If you feel energetic, you are ready to do work. Your muscles have energy stored in them. It comes from the food you eat. Water at the top of a dam has energy. As it falls over the dam, its energy is released. Wood and gasoline have energy too, which they release when heated.

PORKING OUT ON CHOCOLATE CHIP COOKIES IS NOT THE BEST WAY TO STORE UP ENERGY, SIR.

Energy Crisis

When we speak of the energy crisis we mean that the world is in danger of running short of cheap fuel. There is still a lot of fuel on earth, but not as much as there once was. And it is getting very expensive to recover. Also, world politics has caused fuel prices to keep going up and up.

The energy crisis will be solved in two ways. People must stop wasting energy. They also will have to use new kinds of energy. The best answer is to find energy sources that won't run out for a very long time.
See Conservation; Renewable Energy Source

Energy Management

Energy management means saving energy. It is a kind of conservation. When fuels were very cheap, energy management was not very important. But now fuels are expensive. And they are getting more expensive all the time. So energy management is getting a great deal of attention. Maybe your house has a special thermostat that turns down the heat at night. That is a good example of energy management. Can you think of any others?

See Conservation

Engine

An engine is any machine that changes energy into work. An automobile engine changes the chemical energy in gasoline into mechanical work. This work turns the car's wheels. A steam engine burns fuel to make steam. The steam can drive a train or run a power station. Without engines we would have to use animal power — or human power — for all our work!

Environmental Protection Agency

The Environmental Protection Agency (EPA) is a U.S. government agency that fights pollution. It was formed in 1970. The EPA makes laws against pollution. It also fines factory owners and other people who do not obey these laws. So America is getting cleaner. But such laws make energy cost more. They also slow down the building of new power plants, especially nuclear power plants.

See Pollution

Ericsson, John

John Ericsson is best known for building the warship *Monitor* during the American Civil War. But he also invented an engine that ran on energy from the sun.

Ericsson was born in Sweden in 1803. At age 36 he came to the United States, where he built many solar engines for pumping water. In the 1800s wood and coal were so cheap that people were satisfied to run engines with those fuels. No one needed the sun for energy. Now we do. So we are finally getting interested in solar engines like John Ericsson's.

See Solar Energy

Fahrenheit, Gabriel Daniel

Gabriel Fahrenheit (FAIR-en-hite) was born in Prussia in 1686. He is best known for inventing a temperature scale for thermometers. People sometimes think he invented the thermometer. He didn't, but he did make it better. Long ago, thermometers used alcohol. Fahrenheit put mercury in the glass tube instead. Mercury freezes at a very low temperature and boils at a very high temperature. So it can measure a wider range of temperatures than alcohol can.

On Fahrenheit's scale, the number 32 marks the freezing point of water. (So 0 on the scale is 32 degrees below freezing.) The number 212 marks the boiling point of water. Normal body temperature is 98.6 degrees on Fahrenheit's scale. This scale is different from the Celsius scale (which is also for mercury thermometers) used in most countries and in scientific work everywhere.
See Celsius

Fallout

Fallout is a shower of radioactive dust caused by the explosion of an atomic bomb. This dust can travel with the wind for thousands of miles. The cloud can last for days. Fallout harms humans and animals. It also can ruin farmland. Dangerous fallout is one of the reasons people keep trying to outlaw atomic bombs.
See Atomic Bomb; Radioactivity

FALLOUT OR FALL OFF, I GUESS THEY'RE ALL POTENTIALLY DANGEROUS.

HEE HEE HEE

THUD

Fermi, Enrico

Enrico Fermi produced the first nuclear chain reaction. He was born in Rome, Italy, in 1901. As a nuclear scientist, he discovered a new atomic particle and named it a neutrino (new-TREE-no). Fermi received the 1938 Nobel prize in physics for this discovery. He came to America that same year. He was asked to make a chain reaction of radioactive material, the first step toward an atomic bomb. In 1942, in a laboratory at the University of Chicago, he created the first atomic chain reaction. By 1945, the first atomic bomb was successfully exploded.

Enrico Fermi died in 1954. The following year a new man-made element was named fermium to honor him.

See **Atomic Bomb; Atom Splitting; Chain Reaction; Element (Chemical); Radioactivity**

Fire. See Combustion

Flat-Plate Solar Collector

A flat-plate solar collector gathers heat from the sun. It is usually placed on the roof of a building, often with many others like it. If you sliced open a collector, it would look something like this:

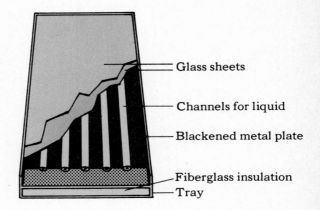

- Glass sheets
- Channels for liquid
- Blackened metal plate
- Fiberglass insulation
- Tray

When the sun shines on a collector, the collector gets very hot. So does the water or air flowing through it. Pipes lead from the collector into the building. A collector may heat water for showers, washing clothes, and doing dishes. Or it may heat a whole building. The temperature of a flat-plate collector reaches to about 150° to 200°F (66° to 94°C). For higher temperatures, a concentrating solar collector must be used.

See Concentrating Solar Collector

Fossil

A fossil is what is left of an animal or plant that lived long ago. Museums have many fossils on display. Coal is the fossil remains of ancient plants. That's why coal is called a fossil fuel. Sometimes we jokingly call an old-fashioned person a fossil. But we don't joke very much about our shrinking supply of fossil fuels.

See **Fossil Fuels**

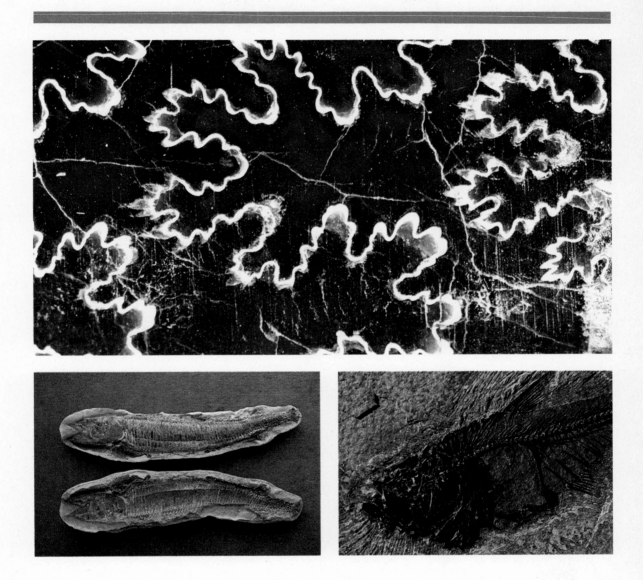

Fossil Fuels

Fossil fuels come from the remains of long-dead plants and animals. Oil, coal, and natural gas are fossil fuels. They took many millions of years to form. First the plants or animals rotted over a long time. Then floods covered the rotted material. Rocks and earth pressed down on the material. And finally it became fossil fuel.

We have used up much of the earth's supply of fossil fuels. Unfortunately, we can't wait millions of years for nature to make more.

See Coal; Natural Gas; Oil

Franklin, Benjamin

Ben Franklin was a famous American born in Boston, Massachusetts, in 1706. He was one of seventeen children. His father was a poor candlemaker. But Ben became rich and famous. He was a printer, a statesman, and a scientist. He invented bifocal eyeglasses and also the Franklin stove.

This kind of stove looks like a fireplace but it is not a fireplace. It is a stove made of cast iron, closed on all sides. Not all the heat it produces goes up the chimney. Instead, much of it moves out into the room the stove is in. So a Franklin stove warms the room well. Franklin stoves are popular today with people who want to save money on fuel.

Franklin flew a kite in a thunderstorm. Electricity coming down the string proved that lightning was the same as manmade electricity. The lightning rod that protects buildings from lightning was also Franklin's invention.

Fuel

Fuel is something used to produce heat or power, usually by burning it. Wood is a fuel. So are gasoline and natural gas. Without fuel, our homes would be cold in winter. Our cars wouldn't run. Neither would our TVs, radios, toasters, and computers.

Fuel Cell

A fuel cell is a special kind of electric battery. There are two types. Both need hydrogen and oxygen gases to generate a current of electricity. The hydrogen and oxygen also join to form water.

The first type of fuel cell is small. Hydrogen and oxygen are put directly into the cell. Some spacecraft use such a fuel cell to produce electric power. And the astronauts drink the water from it!

The second type of fuel cell may soon be used to generate electricity for towns and cities. This large fuel cell uses air and fuel to produce the hydrogen and oxygen the cell needs to generate electricity.

Besides water, this kind of fuel cell gives off the gas carbon dioxide. Neither of these things causes pollution. So a fuel cell is a clean way to generate electricity. It is also a quiet way.

See Electric Battery

G

Gasohol

Gasohol is a mixture of gasoline and alcohol. It is used to power automobiles and trucks. The alcohol is made from corn, sugar cane, and many other plants. This saves some gasoline. Gasohol in the United States is only 10 percent alcohol. But in Brazil, gasohol is 20% alcohol. By the year 2000, Brazil plans to use all alcohol and no gasoline. Because the alcohol is made from plant crops, the supply will never run out like gasoline will. Each year there will be new crops to turn into alcohol.

See Biomass; Renewable Energy Sources

Gas Research Institute

The Gas Research Institute (GRI) looks for better ways to produce and use gas in the USA. This includes natural gas and manmade gas. GRI was started in 1976.

Geiger, Hans

Hans Geiger invented the Geiger counter that detects and measures the strength of nuclear radiation. He was born in Germany in 1882. After college he went to England to work with scientist Ernest Rutherford. In 1913 Geiger invented a machine that counted radiation particles. The machine is called a Geiger counter. People who look for uranium to mine use Geiger counters. The clicking sound the counter makes tells where the uranium ore is.

See Atomic Bomb; Nuclear Radiation; Rutherford, Ernest; Uranium

Geophysicist

Geo means earth. Physics is the study of matter and energy. So a geophysicist (jee-oh-**FIZ**-uh-sist) is a person who studies the matter and energy on and under the surface of our earth. Because of the energy crisis, geophysicists are very important. They search for new supplies of coal, oil, and natural gas. And they find better ways to get these materials out of the earth.

49

Geopressured Gas

Geopressured (JEE-oh-presh-urd) gas is natural gas under pressure deep in the earth. The gas is being squeezed by the rock and sand around it. The squeezing forces the gas up to the surface. It does not need to be pumped.

Geothermal Energy

Geothermal (jee-oh-THUR-mul) energy is the heat in rocks far below the earth's surface. Water is heated by these hot rocks. And sometimes the water turns to steam. When this steam explodes above the earth's surface, we call it a geyser (GUY-zur). Old Faithful in America's Yellowstone Park is the most famous of all geysers. We enjoy looking at it. But geothermal energy can be put to use.

Geothermal steam has been used in Italy since about 1900 to run an electric power plant. There is also a geothermal steam power plant in California called The Geysers. Electricity from it is used in San Francisco. Geothermal energy heats water for homes in Idaho and in Iceland.
See Yellowstone National Park

The Geysers

Old Faithful

Gilbert, William

William Gilbert is called the Father of Electricity. He was born in Essex, England, in 1540. He studied medicine in college and became doctor to Queen Elizabeth I. He also studied and wrote about electricity. The name gilbert was given to a measure of magnetic force.

When the Queen heard that her doctor was called "The Father of Electricity," she was shocked.

I GUESS NOT...

Dr. William Gilbert shows his electricity experiments to Queen Elizabeth I.

Goddard, Robert Hutchings

Robert Goddard was the first man to launch rockets successfully. He was born in Massachusetts in 1882. He was interested in science, and taught it after finishing college. As a teen-ager, he had become interested in rockets. He patented two rocket inventions before he was 22 years old. And he was already thinking about sending rockets to the moon.

In 1923, Goddard tested the first liquid-fuel rockets. Later he launched even bigger rockets. But the American government paid no attention to his work. When World War II came, the Germans had much bigger rockets and almost won the war. Goddard died in 1945. So other Americans (and some Germans too) had to complete Goddard's dream of sending rockets to the moon.

See **Rocket**

Greenhouse

A greenhouse is a building or room made mostly of glass or clear plastic. It lets in the sun's heat and then keeps it in. You can grow flowers and vegetables all winter in a greenhouse. Besides keeping plants warm and getting sunlight to them, the greenhouse protects them from wind and snow.

Today people are building greenhouses onto their homes for a reason that has nothing to do with plants. The greenhouse is a pleasant room in winter, and it can help heat the rest of the house, too. All the greenhouse owner has to do is let heated air flow from the greenhouse into other rooms.

Halflife

The halflife of a radioactive material is the time it takes for the radiation to drop to half of what it was at first. Some radioactive materials have very short halflives. But some have halflives of billions of years! Usually, about ten halflives must pass before the radioactive material is safe to touch. This is why nuclear materials must be handled so carefully.

Here's an example. Suppose your glove was just exposed to nuclear radiation. The glove has become radioactive. Let's say it would take 2 years for the glove's radioactivity to drop to half of what it is now. So it will be 20 years (10 x 2 = 20) before you can safely touch that glove again.

See Nuclear Radiation; Radioactivity

Heat Energy

Heat is a very important form of energy. In the United States about 60 percent of the energy people use is heat. It warms homes and buildings. Heat engines drive generators that produce electricity. Heat operates pumps and other machines. And most of our automobiles run on the heat energy they get by burning gasoline. Without heat energy we would have to work a lot harder to get things done. And we'd freeze too!

Heat energy may be measured in Btu's (British thermal units).

See Btu; Carnot, Nicolas Léonard Sadi

Heavy Water. See Deuterium

Heliostat

A heliostat (HEE-lee-uh-stat) is a large mirror that reflects sunlight onto a solar collector. In order for the collector to do the best possible job, it needs as much sunlight as it can get. So a clockwork is used to move the mirror, keeping it facing directly toward the sun.

A solar power tower uses many heliostats to aim lots of sunlight at a boiler on top of the tower. The sunlight heats the water in the boiler, changing it into steam. The steam drives an electric generator. Someday soon we may all use power towers. They will turn solar energy into electricity for our homes and factories.

See Electric Generator; Power Tower; Solar Collector

Henry, Joseph

Joseph Henry was an American scientist who invented the electric motor and the telegraph (a machine that sends electric signals through wires). Henry was born in Albany, New York, in 1797. He first worked for a watchmaker. Then he became interested in electricity.

Besides inventing the motor and telegraph, Henry discovered the scientific law that came to be called induction. Changing the strength of a current in a coil of wire will make a current flow in a nearby coil, even though no batteries are used.

Knowing about induction, electrical engineers were able to build transformers. A transformer uses two coils of wire to change the voltage, or electrical pressure, of an electric current.

The unit of measurement of electrical induction is called a henry.

See Electric Current; Transformer; Voltage

Joseph Henry

Hiroshima. See Atomic Bomb

Horsepower

Horsepower is a unit used to describe how powerful an engine is. James Watt was the first person to use the term. He used it to compare the power of a steam engine with the power of horses.
See Kilowatt; Watt, James

James Watt compared the power of a steam engine with the power of horses.

Hydrocarbons

Hydrocarbons are chemicals made up of hydrogen and carbon. Fuels such as wood, coal, oil, and gas are hydrocarbons. Carbohydrates—sugars and starches—are also made of carbon and hydrogen. So hydrogen and carbon are used as fuel for machines and for our bodies too!

The Grand Coulee Dam and its power plants generate hydroelectric power.

Hydroelectric Power

Hydroelectric (hye-droe-uh-LECK-trick) power comes from a flow of water. Long ago, flowing rivers turned mill wheels to grind flour. Modern hydroelectric power comes from water falling over a dam. The force of the water turns electric generators that are connected to water wheels called turbines. Much of our electricity comes from these generators.

But you can really thank the sun for hydroelectric power. Here's why: Heat from the sun evaporates water in the ocean and makes clouds. Rain from the clouds fills rivers and lakes with water. This water flows over dams to drive the hydroelectric generators. So hydroelectric power is really solar power. It won't run out like fossil fuels will, and it won't pollute the air either.

See Electric Generator; Turbine

Hydrogen

Hydrogen is the lightest chemical element. At ordinary temperatures it is a gas and burns very cleanly. Some engineers consider it the perfect fuel.

Hydrogen combines chemically with oxygen to make water. It also combines with carbon to produce hydrocarbon fuels and carbohydrate foods. So hydrogen is a very useful element.

See Element (Chemical); Fuel; Hydrocarbons

Hydrogen Bomb

A hydrogen bomb is more powerful than an atomic bomb. In fact, an atomic bomb is used just to set off a hydrogen bomb. The atomic explosion causes atoms of hydrogen in the bomb to join together, or fuse. This nuclear fusion causes a much greater explosion than in atomic bombs exploded by the splitting, or fission, of atoms.

The first hydrogen bomb was tested in 1952 by the United States. It was dropped on Eniwetok (en-uh-WEE-tahck) in the Pacific Ocean. A few years later the Russians exploded a test hydrogen bomb of their own. Fortunately, hydrogen bombs have not been used in wars. They would do far more damage than the atomic bombs did at Hiroshima and Nagasaki during World War II.

See Atomic Bomb; Nuclear Fission; Nuclear Fusion

57

Infrared Radiation

Infrared (in-fruh-RED) radiation is sometimes called heat radiation. It is part of sunlight. We cannot see it, but we can feel it. Solar energy is about half infrared energy. A hot stove gives off lots of infrared radiation too.

See Heat Energy; Solar Energy

Insulation. See Conduction of Heat

International Atomic Energy Agency

The International Atomic Energy Agency (IAEA) was formed in 1956. It was set up in order to increase the use of atomic energy for peaceful purposes. IAEA also tries to stop the use of nuclear weapons.

Today, more than 100 nations belong to IAEA.

International Solar Energy Society

The International Solar Energy Society (ISES) is a group of scientists, engineers, and other people interested in solar energy. The society was formed in 1955 to put solar energy to work. ISES members meet each year to report new ways of using solar energy.

See Solar Energy

Jet Propulsion

Jet propulsion (pruh-PUHL-shun) is what makes jet planes fly. The first airplanes had blades called propellers on their engines. In 1941, Frank Whittle of England made an airplane without a propeller. Gas burned in the jet engine pushed the plane along like a rocket.

Jet propulsion was first used in World War II fighter planes. Jet planes fly higher and faster than propeller planes.

See **Rocket; Whittle, Frank**

Joule, James Prescott

James Joule (JOOL) was a scientist who was interested in electricity and heat. He was born in England in 1818 where he studied science. Once he measured the temperature of a waterfall. As he suspected, the water at the bottom was warmer than the water at the top. The energy of the falling water was changed to heat as it hit the bottom.

Joule measured the heat energy produced by electric current flowing through a wire. He also found out exactly how much mechanical work could be done by a certain amount of heat. In his honor, a unit of work, or energy, is called a joule. One joule is enough energy to lift a 1-pound weight about 9 inches.

See **Thompson, Benjamin**

James P. Joule with one of his experiments

Kilowatt

A kilowatt is 1,000 watts of power. This is equal to about 1⅓ horse-power. Five kilowatts or more of electric power is needed to run the lights and appliances of a modern American home.
See Horsepower; Megawatt; Watt

Kinetic Energy

Kinetic energy is the energy of anything in motion. The turning wheels of your automobile have kinetic energy. So do your legs when you run. Wind has kinetic energy too. It can turn windmills that gener-ate electric power.
See Potential Energy

Langley, Samuel Pierpont

Samuel Langley almost succeeded in inventing the airplane before the Wright brothers did. He was also a pioneer solar scientist. He was born in Massachusetts in 1834. He did not go to college but learned enough to get a job at Harvard University. He became an astronomer. Langley was especially interested in the sun. To measure its radiation he invented a machine called the bolometer.

In 1887 Langley became secretary of the Smithsonian Institution. He studied birds, and began to design an airplane. He had several built. But none was able to fly. Langley was disgraced. The newspapers said humans would never be able to fly. But in 1903 the Wright brothers flew their airplane at Kittyhawk, North Carolina.

Langley is honored in the use of his name as a measure of solar radiation.

See Solar Constant

Antoine Lavoisier in his laboratory

Lavoisier, Antoine

Antoine Lavoisier (luh-VWAH-zee-ay) was a pioneer French solar scientist. He lived from 1743 to 1794.

Lavoisier built a very big solar furnace. He used large glass lenses (curved pieces of glass) to focus sunlight onto a tiny spot. Lavoisier's solar furnace reached temperatures as high as 2,000°C. He actually burned a diamond in it. That was an expensive way of proving how hot his furnace was!

Lavoisier wasn't burning things in his solar furnace for fun. Until then, scientists had thought heat was a substance called phlogiston (floe-JISS-tun), found inside everything, that could be burned. Lavoisier proved there was no such thing as phlogiston.

Sadly, Lavoisier was beheaded during the French Revolution. Those who killed him said France had no need for scientists. *See* **Solar Furnace**

Lignite

Lignite is a fossil fuel on its way to becoming coal. Over the ages, rotted plants changed slowly. First they became a kind of soil called peat. After millions of years, peat became lignite. Lignite is a poor grade of coal sometimes called brown coal. But it is used as fuel because poor fuel is better than no fuel at all.
See **Coal; Fossil Fuels**

Matter and Energy

Matter and energy are different forms of the basic "something" that makes up the universe. Anything that takes up space is matter. But matter is sometimes called frozen energy. This means that there is energy locked up or frozen in everything. Atom splitting is one way to let out the energy that is in matter. An atomic bomb can turn a little bit of matter into a lot of energy.

See Atomic Bomb; Atom Splitting; Einstein, Albert; Nuclear Energy

Mechanical Energy

There are two kinds of mechanical energy. One shows up as work done by a force. An example is lifting a weight against gravity—as when someone jacks up a car. The other kind of mechanical energy is the energy of a moving object. An example of that is the energy of a speeding bullet. The engine in your car has this kind of energy, too.

The world is full of various types of machines. And they all depend on mechanical energy.

Megawatt

A megawatt is one million watts of electric power. This is enough to supply about 250 homes. Some electric power plants produce more than 1,000 megawatts. That much power takes care of a whole city.

See Power; Watt, James

Meltdown

When a nuclear reactor gets too hot and its fuel melts, we say there has been a meltdown. This can happen when both the control rods and the reactor's emergency cooling system fail.

A meltdown is very dangerous. When radioactive fuel melts, harmful radioactive materials can easily escape from the reactor. Scientists thought that the nuclear reactor at the Three Mile Island (Pennsylvania) power plant might melt down when it went out of control in 1979.

See Nuclear Reactor; Radioactivity

Three Mile Island

Methane

Methane is a gas made when tiny living things called bacteria (back-TEER-ee-uh) feed on plant matter, garbage, or manure. Methane can be used as a fuel. It is a chemical combination of hydrogen and carbon. So it is a hydrocarbon fuel like natural gas.

There are millions of small methane gas generators in the world. Most of them are in China and India. But some are in other countries, including the United States. The gas they make can be used for cooking, heating, and generating electricity.

See **Biomass; Bioconversion; Fossil Fuels; Hydrocarbons; Natural Gas**

Minerals

Minerals are nonliving materials found in the earth's crust. Salt, sand, stone, and metallic ores such as iron ore and copper ore are minerals. So is water! Minerals were made as the earth was formed. Many minerals are taken from the earth by mining.

See Coal Mining

N

Nagasaki. See Atomic Bomb

National Coal Association

The National Coal Association (NCA) in Washington, D.C., was started in 1917 to help produce more coal for America. NCA looks for better ways to mine coal and to cut down the air pollution that comes from burning coal. The Association also gives out information about coal and its uses.

See Coal

WHAT COULD A DOG FIND SO INTERESTING IN A NEWSPAPER?

COAL WENT UP FIVE POINTS TODAY. I'LL INFORM MY BROKER TO BUY.

Natural Gas

Natural gas is a fossil fuel. People take it out of the earth by drilling deep holes. Because natural gas was formed in the same way that oil was, oil-well drillers often find the gas on top of or mixed with oil deposits.

People use natural gas for heating and cooking. It is the cheapest of the fossil fuels. It burns very cleanly and causes little pollution. However, it can cause fires and explosions. So we must be careful when using it. Natural gas has no smell. So a gas that smells something like garlic is added. Then if gas is leaking, people can detect it and stop the leak.

Natural gas is a very good fuel. But we will probably use up the earth's supply of it by the year 2000.

See Fossil Fuels; Hydrocarbons

Neutron

Neutrons are tiny particles found in the nucleus, the core, of atoms. When an atom is split, neutrons are released. These neutrons smash more atoms, and can cause a nuclear chain reaction.

See Atom; Atom Splitting; Chain Reaction; Nucleus (Atomic)

Newcomen, Thomas

Thomas Newcomen improved the steam engine invented earlier by Thomas Savery. Newcomen was born in England in 1663. His first job was as a blacksmith. But his real interest was in steam engines. So Newcomen and Savery became partners. Together they made better steam engines than anyone else. The Savery-Newcomen engines were used to pump water in English mines for more than 50 years. Then the even better steam engines of James Watt took over.

See Savery, Thomas; Watt, James

Newton, Isaac

Newton was a scientist who discovered the law of gravity and the laws of motion. He was born in England in 1643. As a child he did not seem very smart. He was not very good at college work either. But later, at his mother's farm, he saw an apple fall from a tree. Newton began to wonder what caused it to fall. In finding out, he realized that there must be a force that makes every object in the universe pull on every other object. He reasoned that this would explain the fall of the apple and also the motion of the planets around the sun. He was right. This force is what we call gravity.

Next Newton discovered the laws of motion. These laws describe how an object moves when forces act on it.

Newton also discovered that sunlight is made up of all the colors of the rainbow. He invented a reflecting telescope, too. This kind of telescope uses a mirror instead of a lens.

See Einstein, Albert

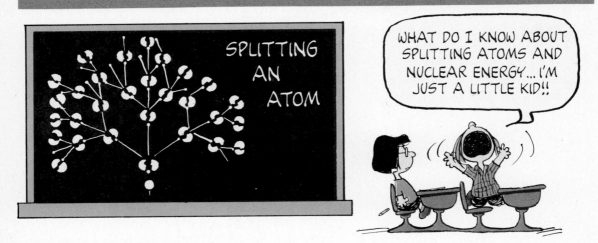

Nuclear Energy

Nuclear (NEW-klee-ur) energy is what holds atoms together. When an atom is split, nuclear energy is released. It is the most powerful energy we know of.

See Atom

Nuclear Fission

Nuclear fission is the splitting of an atom's nucleus. Usually, when this happens two smaller pieces are produced. These pieces, as well as others that result, have tremendous energy. This can be used to make an atomic bomb. Or, if this energy is controlled, it can be changed to heat to run an electric power plant.

See Atom; Nuclear Fusion; Nuclear Power Plant; Nucleus (Atomic); Radioactivity

Nuclear Fusion

When the nuclei (more than one nucleus) of two atoms join together, or fuse, they make a different kind of atom. This fusion (FYOO-zhun) of atoms also produces a lot of energy.

Nuclear fusion is going on in the sun all the time. Atoms of hydrogen combine to form atoms of helium. And energy pours out of the sun to keep us warm and to light up the world. Scientists are trying to make a nuclear fusion power plant here on earth. However, there are still problems of controlling the energy released.

See Atom; Nuclear Fission; Nuclear Power Plant; Nucleus (Atomic)

Nuclear Nonproliferation Treaty

The Nuclear Nonproliferation (non-proe-liff-uh-RAY-shun) Treaty is a pledge by many countries not to use atomic bombs for war. Since the treaty was drawn up in 1968, no country has exploded atomic bombs in a war. This is a good thing, because modern atomic bombs are much more powerful than those dropped in World War II on Hiroshima and Nagasaki in Japan.

See Atomic Bomb

Nuclear Power Plant

A nuclear power plant "burns" a radioactive fuel, uranium, to run a steam-electric generator. The electricity from a nuclear power plant is, of course, just like the electricity from a coal or oil power plant. There are nearly a hundred nuclear power plants in the United States.

A nuclear plant has a nuclear reactor that produces heat from the fission of uranium. The heat turns water in a boiler to steam. The steam runs an electric generator. For safety, the power plant has a cooling system and a heavy concrete shield that covers the reactor. The concrete shield protects people in or near the nuclear power plant in case the reactor should melt down. It also keeps anyone from purposely damaging the reactor.

See Meltdown; Nuclear Fission; Nuclear Reactor; Uranium

Trojan nuclear power plant near Rainier, Oregon

Nuclear Radiation

Nuclear radiation is a stream of energy escaping from radioactive atoms that are splitting. This stream of energy is made of invisible particles called alpha, beta, and gamma rays.

Nuclear radiation can cause sickness or even death to a person exposed to it. The radiation may also harm the children he or she might later have. Some nuclear radiation last for thousands of years. So if we pollute the earth with atomic bombs or nuclear waste from power plants, life will be in danger for a long, long time.

See Atom Splitting; Halflife; Nuclear Waste; Radioactivity

Nuclear Reactor

A nuclear reactor is a furnace that "burns" radioactive fuel such as uranium. Heat comes from the reactor's core, where the uranium fuel is kept in hollow rods. The uranium atoms keep splitting to produce great heat. To keep the core from getting too hot and melting down, control rods are added. The purpose of the rods is something like that of the gas pedal in a car. They keep the core going at the right speed. There is also an emergency core cooling system in case the control rods don't work. This emergency system is like the brakes that keep a car from crashing into something.

A nuclear reactor inside a power plant

Water travels through the reactor and is heated. It turns to steam and then leaves the reactor. In a power plant this steam runs an electric generator.

Most nuclear reactors are used in nuclear power plants. But some are used to produce new radioactive material or for testing new ideas in nuclear energy.

See Meltdown; Nuclear Power Plant; Uranium

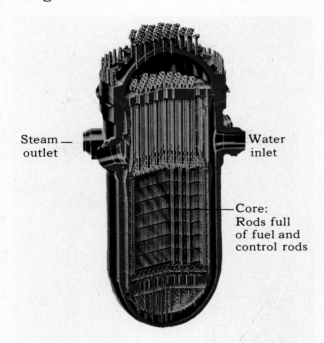

Steam outlet

Water inlet

Core: Rods full of fuel and control rods

Here's what the reactor would look like if it were sliced down the middle.

Nuclear Regulatory Commission

The Nuclear Regulatory Commission (NRC) controls the use of nuclear energy in the United States. It approves all new power plants. It also investigates nuclear accidents. The NRC is all that is left of the old Atomic Energy Commission.
See Atomic Energy Commission

Nuclear Waste

Nuclear waste is what is left when nuclear fuel is burned to make power or weapons. Such waste gives off dangerous, long-lasting radiation.

There seems to be no completely safe way to store nuclear wastes. Many of them leak into the air, the ground, and the water we drink.
See Atomic Bomb; Halflife; Nuclear Radiation; Radioactivity

Nuclear Weapons

The first nuclear weapons were atomic bombs. Then came the much more powerful hydrogen bombs. Now there are neutron bombs that could kill people but leave nonliving things unharmed.

Nuclear weapons can be fired from the ground, from aircraft, or from surface ships and submarines.
See Atomic Bomb; Hydrogen Bomb; Nuclear Nonproliferation Treaty

Nucleus (Atomic)

The nucleus is the heavy center, or core, of an atom. It holds in place the electrons that make up the outer part of the atom. The tiny nucleus itself is made up of even tinier particles called protons and neutrons.
See Atom; Electron; Neutron

Ocean Thermal Energy Conversion

The word thermal means heat. The word conversion means change. Ocean thermal energy conversion changes heat energy from the ocean into useful work. It uses ocean heat to run an engine. The ocean covers almost three-fourths of the earth. So most of the sun's heat falls on the ocean and warms it. This heat could take care of many of our energy needs. But we must find a way of taking it out of the water. That's why scientists are interested in ocean thermal energy conversion (OTEC).

In 1929 the French inventor Georges Claude built an OTEC power plant in Cuba. It did not work well. But the recent energy crisis has made scientists look at the OTEC idea again. In 1979 a small OTEC test plant ran in the ocean near Hawaii. By 1990 large OTEC plants may be working in many places around the world.

OTEC works 24 hours a day, whether or not the sun is visible. And as we take heat energy from the ocean, the sun puts more into it!
See D'Arsonval, Jacques Arsène

Ohm, George Simon

George Simon Ohm was a pioneer electrical scientist. He was born in 1787 in Bavaria (Germany). His father was an engineer, and young Ohm became a science teacher in high school. He also began to do electrical experiments. In 1827 he discovered what is called Ohm's Law. This law tells how much electric current will flow through a wire of a certain size. This is important in the design of electric circuits. The word ohm is used as an electrical measurement in honor of the discoverer of the law.
See Electric Circuit; Electric Current

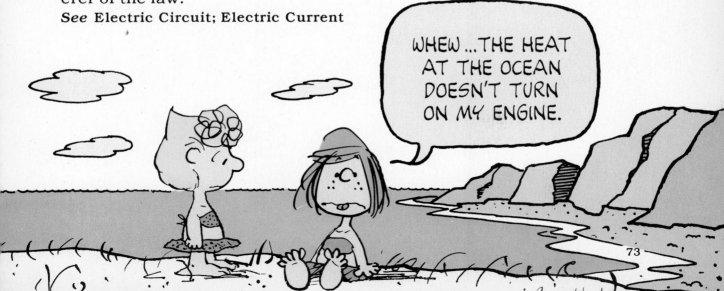

WHEW...THE HEAT AT THE OCEAN DOESN'T TURN ON MY ENGINE.

An oil field

Oil

Oil, or petroleum, is a liquid fossil fuel. It was formed by the rotting of biomass about 600 million years ago. This material was pressed down and heated by rock and earth. Slowly it turned to oil. But the process happened in some places and not in others. And the process has stopped. No new oil is being made. So oil drillers have to look farther and drill deeper every year. The price of oil keeps going up. And someday there won't be any oil left at any price.

See Biomass; Fossil Fuels

An oil refinery seen from an airplane

Oil Field

An oil field is an area where oil is found. This can be on land or under the sea. Oil wells are drilled in many parts of the world. Alaska and the North Sea off Great Britain are examples. So are Venezuela, Saudi Arabia, and Texas and Pennsylvania in the United States. But the amount the United States' oil fields produces is not enough for its needs.

In fact, the United States brings in more oil from other countries than it produces at home.

Oil Refinery

An oil refinery changes crude oil into more useful things. The oil that comes out of an oil well is called crude oil. Oil can work much better when it is changed to other products such as diesel fuel and kerosene. Diesel fuel is used mainly in buses and trucks. Jet engines burn kerosene.

An oil refinery close up

Oil Sands. See Tar Sands

Oil Shale

Oil shale is lightweight rock with oil in it. The United States government plans to make oil from shale.

Shale oil has been produced in small amounts for about 30 years. But it is very expensive, for there is only a little oil in a lot of shale. Huge processing plants will have to be built. And piles of leftover waste will be a problem. We may get lots of oil from shale, but it will cost even more than oil does today.

Oil from oil shale

A plant where oil is removed from oil shale

Oil shale

Oil Tanker

An oil tanker is a very large ship specially built to carry oil. There is no way to get oil across the ocean other than by tanker.

Once in a while a tanker has an accident and oil spills into the ocean. Oil spills are expensive to clean up and the oil kills fish and other ocean life.

Oil Well

An oil well is a hole drilled down into the earth to where the oil is. The first American oil well was only about 60 feet (18 meters) deep. Now some wells are 2 miles (3 kilometers) deep. As an oil well is drilled, a casing, or metal liner, is put in the hole. This is for the oil to flow through. It also keeps rock and dirt from filling up the hole.

Oil wells are very expensive to build and run. And sometimes the drillers don't find any oil. Wells with no oil are called dry holes. Dry holes are often found because there is only a limited supply of oil in the earth. And we have probably found most of it already.

An oil well drill bit has to be changed often.

77

OPEC

OPEC stands for "Oil Producing and Exporting Countries." These countries are:

Algeria	Iran	Libya	Saudi Arabia
Ecuador	Iraq	Nigeria	United Arab Emirates
Gabon	Kuwait	Qatar	Venezuela
Indonesia			

OPEC is very powerful because it owns most of the world's oil. It sets the price of that oil. And it decides how much oil to produce. OPEC's cutback of oil in 1973 led to the "energy crisis" in Europe and North America.
See Energy Crisis

Oxygen

Oxygen is a chemical element that makes up about half of everything on the earth. At ordinary temperatures it is a gas. The air you breathe is 21 percent oxygen. The water you drink is about 90 percent oxygen. And your body is about 65 percent oxygen. Fuel will not burn unless oxygen is present.
See Combustion; Element, Chemical

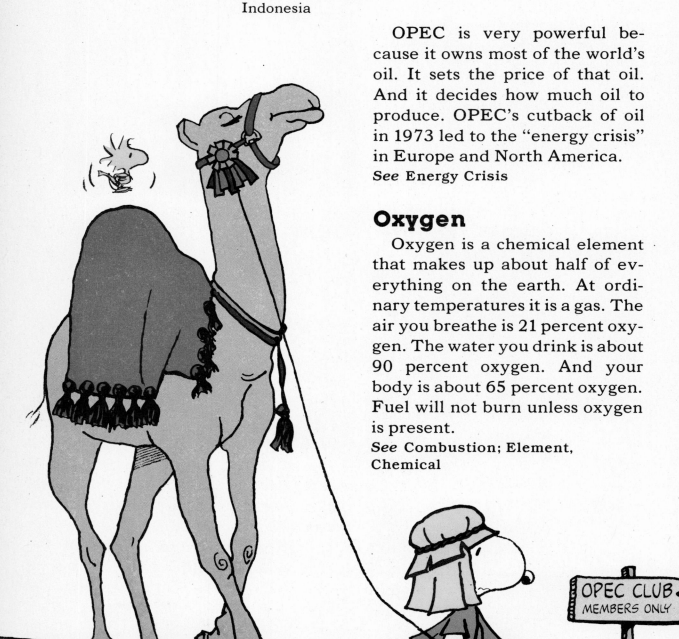

OPEC CLUB
MEMBERS ONLY

Passive Solar Energy

The word passive means doing nothing. The word solar means of the sun. When a house or building by itself is used to change solar energy into heat, we say passive solar energy is at work. A greenhouse is an example of passive solar energy. So is a house that has many windows facing south. Both work as solar collectors. Neither uses pumps, fans, or any other kind of machine.

A greenhouse is an example of passive solar energy.

Indian cliff dwellings are ancient examples of passive solar heating. The winter sun warmed the rock and adobe (clay) buildings. In summer, the overhanging cliff shaded the buildings and kept them cool.

See Greenhouse; Solar Collector

Perpetual-Motion Machines

Perpetual-motion machines are supposed to go on working forever without using any fuel. Don't you believe it! You can't get energy from nothing. Thousands of supposed perpetual-motion machines have been invented. But not one of them has ever done useful work. Unless the laws of nature change, none ever will.

See Work

Petrochemicals

Petrochemicals (PET-roe-KEM-ih-kulz) are chemicals made from oil and natural gas. Petrochemicals include alcohol, ammonia, rubber, plastics, and some detergents. So we depend on oil and gas for a lot more than just fuel.

See Natural Gas; Oil

Petroleum

Petroleum is a fancy name for oil. It comes from two Latin words: *petros*, meaning rock, and *oleum*, meaning oil.

See Oil

Photosynthesis

Photosynthesis (FOE-toe-SIN-thuh-sis) is the way green plants make carbohydrates. It is sometimes called green magic. Water comes up from the soil through the plant's roots to its leaves. And carbon dioxide gas from the air enters the leaves of the plant. When sunlight shines on the leaves, their green coloring matter, called chlorophyll, (KLOHR-uh-fill) soaks up solar energy. This energy changes the water and carbon dioxide to carbohydrates. These are sugars, starches, and cellulose. Sugars and starches are our food. The cellulose is wood and other burnable parts of plants.

Photovoltaic Cell

Photovoltaic (foe-toe-vahl-TAY-ik) cells are batteries that change sunlight to electricity. Sometimes they are called solar batteries. When the sun shines on them, an electric current flows. It is no different from the electric current that comes from the outlet in your home.

Photovoltaic cells were invented in 1954. Yet there are only a few houses in the United States with roofs made of these batteries. The cells are very expensive. But scientists are trying to make cheaper ones. If they succeed, many people may live in homes that get their electric power from the sun.

See Electric Current; Electromagnetic Radiation; Solar Energy

Pipeline

A pipeline is a long metal pipe that carries oil or natural gas across long stretches of land or under water. Such a pipeline carries oil down through Alaska to ports where it is loaded on tankers. Coal can travel through a pipeline too. It is first crushed into a powder and then mixed with water. This mixture is called slurry (SLUHR-ee). A pipeline is a safe, fast, and cheap way to carry fuels.

Planck, Max

Max Planck (PLAHNK) was a German scientist born in 1858. He became a university professor at age 22 and did research in heat energy.

Scientists knew that heat energy moves in waves, something like ocean waves. But Planck thought that energy must be like matter: it must be made up of tiny particles. The size of these particles depended on how much energy was present. Planck called his idea the quantum theory. The word quantum comes from a Greek word meaning how much.

Max Planck

Einstein, Bohr, and other scientists put Planck's idea to the test. They proved that he was right. In his honor the measure of quantum energy is called Planck's Constant. An even greater honor came in 1918 when Planck received the Nobel prize in physics.

See Bohr, Niels; Einstein, Albert; Electromagnetic Radiation

Plutonium

Plutonium is a radioactive material used in atomic bombs. It is produced from uranium in a type of nuclear reactor called a breeder. Many countries are building breeder reactor power plants. But the United States has delayed its breeder program. This is because the government fears the plutonium made in breeder reactors might be used to make atomic bombs.

See Atomic Bomb; Breeder Reactor; Radioactivity; Uranium

Pollution

When something is made unclean, or dirty, it is polluted. Our environment is made unclean, both by nature and by things we do. Pollution comes in various kinds: air, water, and thermal (heat).

When we breathe, we put carbon dioxide into the air. We may also breathe out germs or cigarette smoke. All these things pollute the air. But cars, trucks, and planes pollute it even more. So do fires, factories, and even the dust from farming.

Nature is also an air polluter! Trees give off pollutants called terpenes (TUR-peenz). In 1980 Mount St. Helens, a volcano in the state of Washington, threw tons of rock and ash into the air. Earlier volcanoes poured out enough ash to change the weather over large areas of the earth. But most air pollution is caused when we burn fuel to produce thermal energy.

When we take baths, the ring in the tub shows that we are polluting the water. Wastes from factories, coal mines, and power plants cause much more water pollution.

Thermal pollution heats air or water. This can be bad for the environment. Some power plants have heated rivers so much that fish were cooked!

See Ecology

SPEAKING OF POLLUTION ...

Potential Energy

Potential (puh-TEN-shul) energy is stored energy. It is energy waiting to be used. Water behind a dam has potential energy. When the water falls, the energy becomes kinetic energy—the energy of something in motion. The kinetic energy can run a turbine to make electric power. And so a third kind of energy has been created—electrical energy.

Power Plant

A power plant is a place that holds all the buildings and machinery needed to produce power—often electrical power. A power plant can be run by the energy from fossil fuels, radioactive fuels, or synthetic fuels. Or it can get its energy from the sun, the wind, or water.

See Electric Power; Fossil Fuels; Hydroelectric Power; Nuclear Power Plant; Radioactivity; Synthetic Fuels

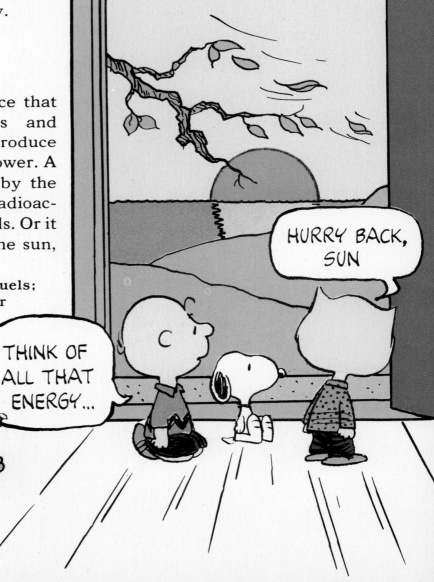

84

Power Tower

A power tower turns solar energy into electrical energy. On top of the tower is a steam boiler with water in it. This boiler is heated by sunlight reflected by hundreds of mirrors. The water turns to steam, like water heated in a kettle on the stove. The steam drives an electric generator. The first large power tower is being built in Southern California.
See Electric Generator

Project Plowshare

In the 1950s, Project Plowshare used nuclear explosions to do peaceful work. This included forcing natural gas from rock far below the ground. The purpose was to do what the Bible says: "...beat their swords into plowshares." (Plowshares are the cutting parts of plows.) This peaceful use of nuclear energy was suggested by the Atomic Energy Commission.
See Atoms for Peace; Natural Gas

Propane

Propane is a gas fuel made from oil. It is used in cigarette lighters. Propane is also mixed with butane gas and compressed in tanks. This bottled gas is used for cooking and for gas lamps.
See Butane; Oil Refinery

Q

Quad

A quad is a unit used to measure very big amounts of heat energy. One quad is equal to a quadrillion Btus of heat energy. A quadrillion is a thousand trillion: 1,000,000,000,000,000! One quad is equal to the energy in about 173 million barrels of oil. The United States used 78 quads of energy in 1979.

See Btu

R

Radiant Energy

Radiant energy is energy that is "radiated," or sent out from something. The sun sends out a tremendous amount of radiant energy. Radiant energy is also called electromagnetic energy.

See Electromagnetic Radiation

Radiation. See Electromagnetic Radiation; Nuclear Radiation

I'VE BEEN SOAKING UP "RADIANT ENERGY" FOR TWENTY MINUTES. DO I LOOK RADIANT?

Radioactivity

Radioactivity is a stream of energy coming from certain materials. The atoms in radium, uranium, and plutonium are radioactive. They keep splitting and sending out energy. Radioactivity is made up of streams of tiny alpha, beta, and gamma particles. Exposure to radioactivity can be dangerous to our health.

See Atom Splitting; Nuclear Radiation; Plutonium; Uranium

Radium

Radium is a shiny white radioactive material. It was discovered by Marie and Pierre Curie. Radium has been used for a long time in treating cancer.

See Curie, Marie and Pierre

Reactor. See Nuclear Reactor

Renewable Energy Source

Renewable energy is the kind that never runs out. The sun, the wind, water power, and wood (we hope!) are renewable energy sources. Someday, renewable sources will give humans all the energy we need.

Rocket

A rocket is a very simple engine. It burns solid or liquid fuel to make a gas that shoots out the back at high speed. That backward force causes the rocket to move forward.

The Chinese made gunpowder rockets for toys many centuries ago. Americans enjoy these kinds of rockets on the Fourth of July. Modern rocket experiments began in 1926. In that year, Robert Hutchings Goddard sent a rocket up about as high as a 26-story building.

In order to burn its fuel, a rocket needs oxygen gas. Chinese rockets took their oxygen from the air. Today's rockets carry their own oxygen so they can propel spacecraft that fly in space, where there is no air.

See Goddard, Robert Hutchings; Whittle, Frank

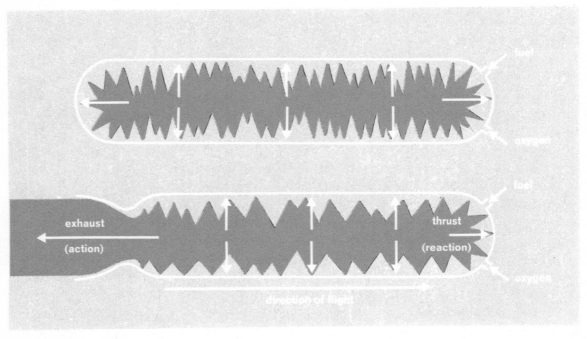

How a rocket works

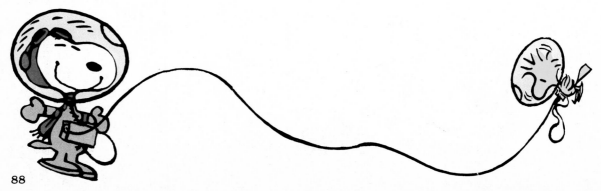

The space shuttle *Columbia* has a total of 67 rocket engines!
Only 3 are the orbiter's main engines.

Roentgen, Wilhelm Konrad

Wilhelm Roentgen (RENT-gen) discovered X-rays. He was born in Prussia in 1845. After studying engineering, he became interested in electromagnetic radiation. One day he experimented with a cathode-ray tube. The tube made a stream of radiation inside its glass walls. But it also produced another kind of radiation. This went right through cardboard and wood. It even went through Roentgen's hand!

He learned that the strange radiation could make a picture of the bones in his hand. Roentgen called his discovery X-rays. He used an X to name the rays because he wasn't quite sure what they were.

Wilhelm Konrad Roentgen

The first Nobel prize in physics was given to him in 1901. And the measurement of X-rays is called a roentgen.

See Electromagnetic Radiation

Rumford, Count. See Thompson, Benjamin

Rutherford, Ernest

Ernest Rutherford was one of the first nuclear scientists. He was born in New Zealand in 1871. But he did his research in England. Rutherford discovered the tiny nucleus, or core, of the atom. In 1908 he received the Nobel prize in chemistry. In 1914 he was knighted by the King of England for his work.

By 1917 Rutherford succeeded in splitting nitrogen atoms, changing them to oxygen atoms. But he died believing that nothing would ever come of his atom splitting. Of course, he was wrong. Nuclear energy is possible only because of atom splitting.

See Atom Splitting; Nuclear Energy; Nuclear Fission

Savery, Thomas

Thomas Savery invented the first successful steam engine. He was born in England in 1650 and began inventing things at an early age. The English coal mines were having trouble with floods. So Savery decided to build a pump to take water out of the mines. He did this with a big steam engine—the first practical one ever built. Savery called his pump the miner's friend. Many such engines were built around 1700. *See* Newcomen, Thomas; Steam Engine

Seebeck, Thomas Johann

Thomas Seebeck was a German scientist who discovered thermo-electricity, electricity produced by heat. He was born in 1770, before much was known about electricity. But he found that when two wires of certain metals were joined at the ends, an electric current flowed. This happened only if the two places where the wires were connected were kept at different temperatures. This so-called Seebeck effect was not used in a practical way for a long time. But now, thermoelectricity has many uses. There are even small thermoelectric refrigerators.

Solar Airplane

A solar airplane flies on solar power. A few years ago, Paul Macready first designed a very light human-powered airplane. It could stay in the air as long as its pilot pedaled! This plane made one flight in California. Then it flew across the English Channel between England and France.

Next, Macready put a panel of photovoltaic cells on the plane. When the sun shines on them, an electric current flows. This electricity was meant to power the plane. In August 1980 a young woman flew Macready's plane using this solar power. No one expects solar power ever to be the main way to power airplanes. But the flight proved that solar energy can do more than many people thought it could.

See Photovoltaic Cells

Janice Brown piloting the world's first totally solar-powered "manned" airplane, the *Gossamer Penguin*

Solar Battery. See Photovoltaic Cell

Solar Collector

A solar collector is any device that captures sunlight and changes it into heat energy. Solar collectors can heat water or buildings. They can also be used to make engines work.

Solar collectors are becoming a common sight on rooftops in the United States. There are now hundreds of thousands of solar collectors. Some are made of glass and have flat black plates under them that get hot. Others use mirrors to concentrate the sun's rays.

See Concentrating Solar Collector; Flat-Plate Solar Collector; Power Tower; Solar Cooker; Solar Furnace

Solar Constant

The solar constant is the average amount of heat energy reaching the earth's atmosphere from the sun. It is usually measured in calories per minute. The solar constant is called a langley in honor of American solar scientist S. P. Langley.

See Calorie; Langley, Samuel Pierpont

Solar Cooker

A solar cooker, or solar stove, uses the sun's heat to cook food. There are two types of solar cookers. One is an oven. In it you can bake cakes and roast meats. The other is a solar hotplate that can make coffee and fry bacon and eggs.

Solar stoves can be bought or built from plans. They are safe to use in camping areas that do not allow open fires. They don't smoke or leave ashes. Also, cooking in the backyard with solar stoves keeps the kitchen cool in summer.

Solar Energy

Solar energy comes to us from the sun. It is actually waves of electric and magnetic radiation that the sun is always sending out. Although only about one two-billionth of the sun's radiation ever reaches the earth, it is enough to give us useful light and heat.

Solar energy is really many kinds of energy. People are using direct solar energy to heat their homes and to run some machines. There is even an airplane run by nothing but solar energy! Energy from the sun also helps wood and other plants used as fuels to grow. And people change some solar energy into electrical energy.

Because some parts of the earth are warmed more than others, solar energy causes the wind to blow. Today some people are catching the energy of wind with windmills. The windmills turn electric generators to produce an electric current.

Hydroelectric power comes from solar energy too. The sun evaporates water, which then gathers to form clouds. Clouds drop rain that fills the reservoirs (REZ-ur-vwahrz) behind dams. The energy of the water flowing over the dams turns electric generators.

We on earth use only a small part of the solar energy that reaches us. Even if we used no other form of energy, there would be more than enough for our needs. And that energy will be available for billions of years—or as long as there are humans to use it.

See **Biomass; Electric Generator; Electromagnetic Radiation; Hydroelectric Power; Windmill**

Solar single point collector

The largest solar furnace in the world

Solar Furnace

A solar furnace is a furnace heated by the sun's energy. Glass lenses or mirrors focus solar heat onto a small area that gets very hot. So users must be very careful not to burn themselves.

The largest solar furnace in the world is in southern France. It is 115 feet (35 meters) high and 165 feet (50 meters) wide. Its mirror covers the side of an entire building! The sun's rays reflect off the building onto a smaller building that gets very hot inside—up to 5,000° F (about 2,800° C). Scientists do experiments using this furnace and also melt metal in it.

You can buy or build a small solar furnace for hobby or craft work. You can use it to solder (SAHD-ur), or join, metals or to bake clay, enamel, or glass jewelry.

See Concentrating Solar Collector; Lavoisier, Antoine

Solar Pond

A solar pond is a body of water heated by the sun. It can be a natural pond or a manmade one. The ponds are heated by the sun. If you put a plastic cover over the water, you can keep most of the heat in. Your solar pond may get so hot that the water boils! You can use the hot water to heat a building or run an engine. Scientists in Israel use solar ponds to generate electricity. Someday they may make Israel's Dead Sea into a giant solar pond!

See Heat Energy

Solar Power Farm

A solar power farm is a place that produces electric power instead of crops. In 1960 some scientists suggested that 5,000 square miles (about 1,300 square kilometers) of desert in the south-western United States be cov-ered with solar collectors. This power farm could generate

A future solar power farm may be covered with solar collectors similar to these.

enough electricity for the whole country. There are no plans right now to build such a large power farm. But a smaller one is now being built in California that will provide electricity for 2,500 homes.
See Power Tower

Solar Power Satellite

Someday most of the energy that people use could come from a solar power satellite. Such a satellite would orbit the earth like a giant space-ship. It would change sunlight to electrical energy. This energy could be changed to electromagnetic energy and beamed through space to the earth.

Building such a solar satellite would cost many billions of dollars. Some people think it may be dangerous because the energy beam might swing off course and harm humans or animals in its path.

SOMETHING ELSE TO WORRY ABOUT...

Solar Still

A solar still makes fresh water from salt water by using energy from the sun. The sun heats the still and evaporates the water in it. Water vapor rises into the air, leaving the salt behind. The vapor condenses, or becomes liquid water again, when it touches the glass cover of the still. The water runs down the glass into a storage tank.

A large solar still was working in Chile about 100 years ago. Today there are many solar stills. Some are very small and make only a few quarts of water a day. But some are quite large. They provide a whole neighborhood with drinking water.

Solid Waste

Solid waste is burnable trash, garbage, and sewage. Many towns and cities now burn solid wastes for fuel. This saves expensive gas and oil. It also gets rid of waste that would otherwise cause pollution. Of course, solid waste must be burned in special furnaces that keep harmful chemicals out of the air.

Steam Engine

A steam engine uses the heat energy in steam to do work. Water is boiled and it turns to steam. In one common type of steam engine, the steam pushes back and forth one or more pieces of metal called pistons. The pistons are attached to a metal rod that moves as the pistons move. This movement can run a train, a steamboat, or a steam-electric generator.

See Newcomen, Thomas; Savery, Thomas; Watt, James

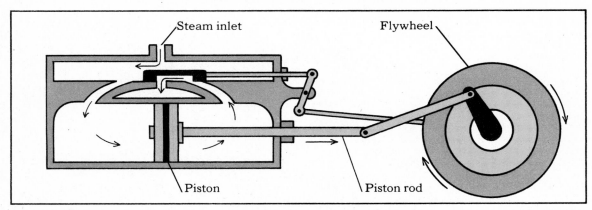

Steam inlet   Flywheel

Piston   Piston rod

Steinmetz, Charles Proteus

Charles Steinmetz was a genius and an electrical wizard. He was born in 1865 in a part of Germany that is now Poland. He moved to Switzerland, and then to the United States. There he went to work as a scientist for the General Electric Company.

Charles Steinmetz

Although Steinmetz was born handicapped—he was a hunchback—he used his talents to become a success. Steinmetz patented more than 200 inventions. And he was famous for creating bolts of lightning in his laboratory. He also showed that alternating current worked better than direct current in electric power plants. That's why we use alternating current for most of our electrical needs.

See Alternating Current; Direct Current

Strip Mining

Strip mining is the digging of coal close to the surface of the earth. It is cheaper than digging a deep mine. But huge strip-mining machines cut up the land as coal is scraped out. Deep scars remain for a long time. So we have new laws that make miners restore the land after they strip-mine it.

Strip mining

Sun

Our sun is a star. It is a type of star that scientists call an orange dwarf. But it is certainly a big dwarf! The sun measures 864,000 miles (1,390,000 kilometers) across. It weighs 2,200 trillion trillion tons! Inside the sun the temperature is about 30 million degrees Fahrenheit (16 million degrees Celsius). Its surface temperature is "only" 10,000 degrees Fahrenheit (6 million degrees Celsius). Scientists think the sun is about 4 billion years old. And it will probably shine for another 4 billion years.

The sun is a giant nuclear reactor. Nuclear fusion inside it changes hydrogen to helium. This produces tremendous amounts of radiant energy. Sunshine falling on the United States each year is equal to the energy of 1,150 billion tons of coal!

See Nuclear Fusion; Nuclear Reactor; Solar Energy

Sunspots

Sunspots look like dark blotches on the surface of the sun. But they are probably huge whirlpools of gas. Sunspots appear, grow, and disappear. Scientists think these changes may affect our weather. We know for sure that they do affect radio communication, and even electric power lines.

Sunspots were first studied by the Italian astronomer Galileo (gal-uh-LEE-oh) with his telescope in 1610. But Chinese astronomers had reported them centuries earlier.

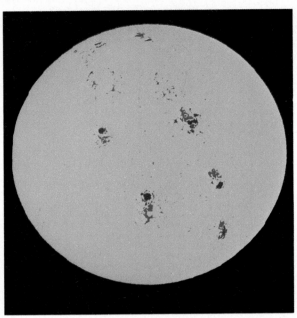

The dark blotches are sunspots.

THIS SHOW IS AWFUL! WHERE ARE THE SUNSPOTS WHEN YOU NEED THEM?

Synthetic Fuels

Synthetic means artificial, or manmade. Synthetic fuels are liquids and gases made from coal or other fossil fuels.

We have a lot of coal in the United States. But coal would be hard to put in the tank of an automobile or to cook with. So liquid and gas fuels are now being made from it. We may be forced to use a lot of synthetic fuels in the near future.

See Fossil Fuels

Tar Sands

Tar sands are made of sandstone with thick crude oil in it. They are sometimes called oil sands. The earth's crust consists of layers of different kinds of minerals. Some of those layers are oil-bearing sands. When oil drillers bring up core samples, they look for these sands. The oil in them could be used for fuel—if we could find an easy way to get it out of the sand.

Tar sands are found in many parts of the world. Canada has about 900 billion barrels of oil in tar sands. South America has 700 billion barrels. The United States has only small amounts of tar sands—mostly in Utah and California. But as this country runs short of oil from underground, it hopes to use oil from these tar sands.
See Core Drilling; Crude Oil

Thermal Pollution. See Pollution

Thermodynamics. See Heat Energy

Thompson, Benjamin

Benjamin Thompson was known as Count Rumford. The Count was the first scientist to prove that heat is a form of motion. He was born in Massachusetts in 1753. During the American Revolutionary War he joined the British army. Later he lived in England, then Bavaria (Germany) and France.

Count Rumford became interested in the science of heat energy. In the 1700s heat was thought to be an invisible thing that moved from one material to another. While making holes in metal, Rumford learned that heat is caused by friction, the rubbing of one thing against another. Rumford worked out a formula that shows how much heat is produced when a given amount of mechanical work is done.
See Joule

WHAT DO I KNOW OF BENJAMIN THOMPSON?

HE WAS A TURNCOAT!!! SORRY, MA'AM, THAT WAS JUST A GUT REACTION.

Thomson, Joseph John

Joseph John Thomson discovered electrons. It is the movement of electrons that creates an electric current.

Thomson was born in England in 1856. He went to Cambridge University to teach. He stayed all his life to do research.

Thomson discovered electrons while he was studying atoms. For this discovery he received the Nobel prize in physics in 1908.

See Atom; Electron

Transformer

A transformer changes the voltage, or force, of an electric current. It uses the induction principle discovered by Joseph Henry. A 110-volt electric supply can be stepped up to 220 volts by a transformer. Or it can be stepped down to 24 volts. This is necessary because different electrical devices are built to use different voltages. Your house probably uses 110-volt electricity. But some houses have large air conditioners that use 220-volt electricity. Some small equipment, such as a toy electric train, doesn't need 110 volts. So a transformer brings that voltage down to whatever voltage is needed.

See Henry, Joseph; Voltage

A transformer

Transmission lines strung on high towers

Transmission Lines

Transmission lines carry electricity from a power plant to homes, offices, stores, and factories. These lines are often strung on huge towers. They go up and down hills, through forests, and over rivers. In cities they are underground, inside pipes or tunnels. In either case, the transmission lines leak some of the energy they carry. This electromagnetic radiation affects radio and TV reception and may be a danger to nearby living things.

See Electromagnetic Radiation

A turbine in a geothermal power plant

Turbine

A turbine (TUR-bin) is a wheel that is turned by the force of air, steam, water, or another fluid. It changes mechanical energy into work. A water wheel is a turbine, and so is a pinwheel. Electric generators are often driven by large steam turbines.

See Electric Generator; Mechanical Energy; Work

Ultraviolet Rays

Ultraviolet rays are part of sunlight that we cannot see. They are so strong they can burn your skin. They can also damage living cells. We are lucky that the earth's atmosphere stops most ultraviolet rays from reaching us. But those ultraviolet rays that get through to the earth are what cause sunburn.

Uranium

Uranium (yoo-RAY-nee-um) is a radioactive material. It gives off nuclear radiation. As it does this, it slowly changes from one chemical element into another and another. Uranium finally becomes lead. Then it is no longer radioactive.

Uranium is fuel for nuclear power plants. Like fossil fuels, it is getting scarce.

See Element, Chemical; Fossil Fuels; Nuclear Power Plant; Nuclear Radiation

Volta, Alessandro

Alessandro Volta invented two important electrical devices. He was born in Italy in 1745. At age 14 he decided to study electricity. His first invention was the electrophorus (ih-leck-TROF-ur-us). This device generated and stored small amounts of electricity. It is still used in laboratories. Now it is called a capacitor.

Volta also invented the electric battery. He made batteries of copper and zinc. They were called voltaic piles.

Napoleon rewarded Volta by appointing him to the Legion of Honor. We honor him every time we use the words volt and voltage.
See Electric Battery; Voltage

Alessandro Volta with a voltaic pile

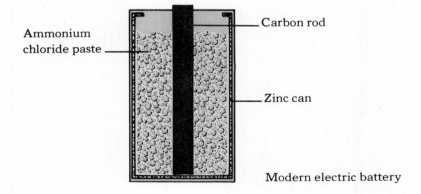

Ammonium chloride paste

Carbon rod

Zinc can

Modern electric battery

Voltage

Voltage is a kind of electrical force, or push, behind an electric current. Our homes generally use 110 volts of electric power. Some foreign countries use 220 volts. So lights and appliances must be designed for the right voltage.
See Transformer

W

Water Pollution. See Pollution

Water Power. See Hydroelectric Power

Watt, James

Many people name James Watt as the inventor of the steam engine. But he did not really invent it. He was born in Scotland in 1736. Steam engines had been invented hundreds of years before. More recently, Thomas Savery and Thomas Newcomen had made steam engines that were being used in pumping water out of mines. Watt designed engines that were more efficient. They produced more energy for each pound of wood or coal burned. So people began using them for many more kinds of work.

To honor Watt, power is measured in watts. Watt also gave us the word horsepower. He used it to tell people how powerful his steam engines were.

See Horsepower; Newcomen, Thomas; Savery, Thomas

A Watt steam-pumping engine at an English coal mine

Wave Power

Wind causes water waves. There is a great deal of power in them. If you have been knocked down by a wave at the beach you know this. For many years engineers have tried to make use of the power of waves. They have built and tested machines that can use wave power. The machines work. But they are damaged by storms.

Whittle, Frank

Frank Whittle invented the jet engine. He was born in England in 1907. As a cadet in the Royal Air Force he dreamed of faster airplanes. In 1930 he patented a jet engine. Before that time, an aircraft engine turned a propeller, which pushed the aircraft forward. In a jet engine a fuel is burned that gives off hot exhaust gases. The gases shoot out the back of the engine in a stream. This stream is called a jet. The jet moving out the rear causes the plane to move forward. A jet engine works something like a rocket, with no need for a propeller.

The British government was slow to use Whittle's jet engine idea. Germans and Italians flew the first jet warplanes in World War II. But it was Frank Whittle who started the jet age. Remember him next time you fly in a jet plane!

See Jet Propulsion; Rocket

Windmill

A windmill uses the energy in wind to do work. The windmill got its name because early wind machines milled, or ground, grain. Later they were used to pump water, and many of them generated electricity. In the early 1900s there were millions of windmills in the United States. Then large electric power plants generated cheap electricity and people didn't need windmills anymore.

In the 1940s a big windmill was built in Vermont to produce electric power for more than 1,000 people. Today, in many countries, there are even larger windmills producing electricity. These do not burn any fuel or cause any pollution. Windmills are coming back into use because gas and oil are growing much more expensive all the time.

See Solar Energy

Work

We say that mechanical work is being done when something is lifted or pushed. If you lift one pound one foot, you have done one foot-pound of work. A ton of coal or a tank of gasoline can do certain amounts of work. How fast a piece of work gets done depends on the power rating of the engine used.

See Energy; Horsepower

I LOVE TO WATCH OTHERS WORK... HEE HEE HEE

X-rays

X-rays are a form of electromagnetic radiation. Because these rays can go right through solid things, they are used to make pictures of the insides of things.

See Electromagnetic Radiation; Roentgen, Wilhelm Konrad

Yellowstone National Park

Yellowstone is the oldest national park in the United States. It covers more than two million acres (20,000 hectares) and has more geysers and hot springs than any other place in the world. These geysers and hot springs are the results of geothermal energy. Heat deep inside the earth raises the temperature of underground water. It comes to the earth's surface as a hot bubbling spring (hot spring) or as an explosion of steam (geyser).
See Geothermal Energy

Zirconium

Zirconium (zur-KOH-nee-um) is a grayish-white metal used to make the cores of nuclear reactors. It is ideal for such use because it does not easily rust and doesn't readily soak up neutrons.

See Neutron; Nuclear Reactor

Index